A WOMAN UNDER THE SURFACE

A Woman Under the Surface

Poems and Prose Poems

by Alicia Ostriker

*for Phyllis Thompson
old friend and
wonderful poet —*

Alicia Ostriker

Princeton University Press
Princeton, New Jersey

Publication of this book has been aided by a grant from the
Paul Mellon Fund of Princeton University Press

This book has been composed in Linotron Sabon

Clothbound editions of Princeton University Press books are
printed on acid-free paper, and binding materials are chosen
for strength and durability

Printed in the United States of America by
Princeton University Press, Princeton, New Jersey

Roll up your sleeve.
There are the veins.

CONTENTS

Acknowledgments   ix

I

The Waiting Room   3
After the Shipwreck   5
The Crazy Lady Speaking   6
The Exchange   7
Fisherman   8
The Raven of Death   9
Camping by the Pacific   10
The Pleiades in December: Line of Sight   11
The End of the Line   12
Ceremony of the Bathtub   13
As in a Gallery   14
In Spring Rain   15
Moon and Earth   16

II

To Kill the Dove   21
Downstairs   23
Ceremony of the Box   24
The Call   25
The Demonstration   26
The Terrorist Trial and the Games   27
This Dreamer Cometh   28
The History of America   29
San Juan Waterfront   30
Those Who Know Do Not Speak, Those Who Speak Do Not
    Know   31
Three Women   32
Two Writers: For J. D.   35
The Long Horn   36
Like Fruit   38

III

Message from the Sleeper at Hell's Mouth 41
The Impulse of Singing 48
Homecoming 49
The Runner 51
Homage to Dante 53
Homage to Matisse 54
Anecdote with Flowers: 1919 56
A Minor Van Gogh (He Speaks): 57
Waterlilies and Japanese Bridge 58
For the Daughters 60

IV

The Diver 63
The Pure Unknown 64
Like an Orphan 65
The Blood 66
Ceremony of Houses 67
Dream: The Disclosure 68
The Voices 69
Dreaming of Her 70
Don't Be Afraid 71
The Courage 72
A Woman Walking in the Suburbs 73
Storm 74
Anxiety about Dying 75
The Singing School 76

A Note on "Message from the Sleeper at Hell's Mouth" 77

ACKNOWLEDGMENTS

Acknowledgment is made to the following publications in which some of these poems have previously appeared: *Hanging Loose, Greenfield Review, Berkeley Poets Cooperative, US 1 Worksheets, California Quarterly, Midwest Quarterly, Beyond Baroque, MS., The Little Magazine, Columbia, Harvard Magazine, Feminist Studies, rara avis,* and *Journal of Popular Culture.*

"To Kill the Dove," "The Impulse of Singing," and "Ceremony of the Box" first appeared in *Canto,* volume 1, number 3.

"Like Fruit" first appeared in *Center.*

"The History of America" first appeared in *Parnassus.*

"The Raven of Death," "The Crazy Lady Speaking," and "Anecdote with Flowers" first appeared in *American Poetry Review.*

"The Blood" first appeared in *Poetry Now.*

"The Pure Unknown" first appeared in *Hudson Review.*

"Fisherman," "After the Shipwreck," "The End of the Line," "Anxiety about Dying," and "Message from the Sleeper at Hell's Mouth" first appeared in *Poetry.*

I

The Waiting Room

We ladies in the Waiting Room of the Atchley Pavilion
Of the Columbia Presbyterian Medical Center
Range in age from the early thirties to the sixties.
We are wearing our tweeds, our rings. The carpet is beige.

Beige walls, beige soundproofed ceilings, beige sofas surround us.
Geometric design of a room divider, wrought iron, to separate
The reception area from the waiting area,
To suggest, gently, that sterility means peace.

Outside, the day is brilliant, windy, and bittercold.
We have come through this weather, but now it does not exist.
We think of our breasts and cervixes.
We glance, shading our eyelids, at each other.

I am wondering what would be a fully human
Way to express our fears, these fears of the betrayal
Of our bodies. How we rely on this machine of flesh:
Dearer than friends, than lovers, than our own thoughts

Can be, it is loyal to us. That without notice it may
Grow subversive seems intolerable, an uprising of house-slaves
Who have always belonged to the family and accomplished
Their tasks discreetly, ever since we were born.

Perhaps we should dress less expensively
And not so well disguise the skeleton. Perhaps
We should sit more closely, ladies, to each other,
On couches arranged to form a circle, upholstered

Some vivid color. Perhaps we should sit on the floor.
They might have music for us. A woman dancer
Might perform, in the center of the circle. What would she do?
Would she pretend to rip the breasts from her body?

From behind a wall, we hear a woman's voice
Screaming. It simply screams. One person
In the waiting room has turned around. Her false
Sooty eyelashes have opened wide.

A few minutes later the screaming has stopped
And the woman in false eyelashes (I see she is very
Pretty, with black long hair, white blouse with bright
Tropical design on sleeves) has lit a cigarette.

After the Shipwreck

Lost, drifting, on the current, as the sun pours down
Like syrup, drifting into afternoon,

The raft endlessly rocks, tips, and we say to each other:
Here is where we will store the rope, the dried meat, the knife,

The medical kit, the biscuits, and the cup.
We will divide the water fairly and honestly.

Black flecks in the air produce dizziness.
Somebody raises a voice and says: Listen, we know there is land

Somewhere, in some direction. We must know it.
And there is the landfall, cerulean mountain-range

On the horizon: there in our minds. Then nothing
But the beauty of ocean,

Numberless waves like living, hysterical heads,
The sun increasingly magnificent,

A sunset wind hitting us. As the spray begins
To coat us with salt, we stop talking. We try to remember.

The Crazy Lady Speaking

I was the one in the IRT tunnel
Rummaging in my patent-leather pocketbook
While deep blue lights flew by the subway window.
You hated my stockings, rolled to the knee.

I was the one in the cafeteria at 2 a.m.
My eyes were flat pennies and stared at your plate.
To you it was worse than India.
You were afraid I might urinate on the floor.

I was the one in the faded sweater
Missing three buttons, my hair dyed pumpkin,
At the baseball game in August,
Yelling behind you, getting spit in your hair.

I have all of the rings and necklaces
I need. My apartment smells of cat.
I want to invite you to it. What I approach
Grows like a jungle. I am the one who loves you.

You should have seen me dance in *La Sylphide*,
In *Lac des Cygnes*. You should have seen
My Cleopatra, my Camille, my Juliet.
From each of their graves I rise, daughter. Embrace me.

The Exchange

I am watching a woman swim below the surface
Of the canal, her powerful body shimmering,
Opalescent, her black hair wavering
Like weeds. She does not need to breathe. She faces

Upward, keeping abreast of our rented canoe.
Sweet, thick, white, the blossoms of the locust trees
Cast their fragrance. A redwing blackbird flies
Across the sluggish water. My children paddle.

If I dive down, if she climbs into the boat,
Wet, wordless, she will strangle my children
And throw their limp bodies into the stream.
Skin dripping, she will take my car, drive home.

When my husband answers the doorbell and sees
This magnificent naked woman, bits of sunlight
Glittering on her pubic fur, her muscular
Arm will surround his neck, once for each insult

Endured. He will see the blackbird in her eye,
Her drying mouth incapable of speech,
And I, having exchanged with her, will swim
Away, in the cool water, out of reach.

Fisherman

Imagine a fisherman in summer deep
Enough to have drowned all other seasons—

His river flows between banks of ash and hickory,
Blackberries ripen, cobwebs form in the shrubs,

Bluejays grow drowsy. Living in his dream,
Having escaped his relatives, a fisherman—

All above water is gauze, hotly in touch, dry light,
A late Monet, a Bach

Chorale, a woman peeling oranges—
Only the cold trout must elude the dream.

Under his boat in the brown flood, pure muscle,
They glide along as if he does not exist,

Like courteous phrases in a dead language.
Their glassy eyes look past each other, hopeless.

It is the way the fisherman wishes. He casts
His line again and again in the heavy heat.

The Raven of Death

A grey November morning. We make love
On our old marriage bed, strong, sweet.

Without a sound, the raven of death
Passes between us a black, serrated wing.

Across the long fields of Jersey and Pennsylvania
Corn stands in yellowed rows.

We are perspiring, pressing together. The raven
Softly lifts to a black dot in the sky.

Camping by the Pacific

Crept from the tent at midnight, out alone
In the dark, where there is nothing to see
And one must depend upon one's ears, heard
The ocean, how she howls, how she roars, how
She moans she would rape the earth masterfully,
Groans she would feed on us, sleep with us, weep with us,
Mourn for us afterward over and over,
Panting and pacified, jealous and never sated.

The Pleiades in December:
Line of Sight

The Pleiades
emitted this
light four
hundred years
ago, it has traveled
at the speed
of light, the shape
composed
has been that
of a curved
pillar
as it
presently arrives
at this frozen
lake

The watery Pleiades
down space, down
time, light
down clear atmosphere
tonight, my cold
nose, sweater, mittens,
knees in pants, dim
two skates standing,
silver gray ice, opaque
jewel gray ice,
black gray ice,
heavy lines,
cracks

water

The End of the Line

Finally the last passengers
Have gotten off the trolley:
A man with hair

The color and texture of damp corn tassels,
Two black women in Lycra
Jackets, maybe a mother and daughter,

And you have passed the tenements,
The boarded warehouses, the auto graveyards.
You say goodnight to the conductor,

He says goodnight, take care.
When you step down, heavy as a stallion,
You find an eighth of an inch of snow,

Fresh and crisp
On the ground, on the pieces of broken pavement,
Plant stubble and ridged mud:

This is lovely, and you did not expect it.
The clear air filled with ice
Particles stings your face,

And when you breathe it hits
Your upper nasal passages like cocaine.
There are no streetlamps, but a full moon lights

The countryside a few miles off.
You wipe your eyes with your glove.
You feel newborn.

A dim red light,
The trolley has started back
When you begin to run.

Ceremony of the Bathtub

The man and his son in the bathtub have a conference
About genitals. The son thinks balls are to make thunder
But he is only six. It is something he heard in nursery school.
The man explains they hold the seeds. The boy inquires what color
The seeds are. When the father says white, the son is relieved
And carouses a bit among the bubbles; he'd thought it was black.

The son is convinced that his penis is too small.
No amount of reassurance will persuade him otherwise.
Father, the hairy bear, immodestly stands and prances.
"Don't look at me," cries the boy. Being looked at drives him to fury.
Father subsides. The boy giggles and splashes. The mother
Slips in and out of the bathroom, adoring his soapy body.

Getting him into the bathtub has been a parental triumph.
Lukewarm water unites the two males now.
The month is July, and an afternoon sky, that pours hotly
And continuously through the bathroom window like a wedge,
Suspending gray dustmotes in the air, striking the porcelain tiles,
Somewhat relaxes the man and his son, helps them forget themselves.

As in a Gallery

As in a gallery, a large posh art gallery, it may happen
Among the footfalls
That you and the wine-mouthed stranger
Look at each other across
The amusing modern construction
With a twinkle: now we are smiling

Conspirators—as in a James Bond movie,
We're in the spacious network, we're the good ones—this occurs
More easily between
Strangers, perhaps, in bars, on exotic travels—
You need give nothing, for it has all been given—but
Rarely with those you love, who are smeared with fear.

Rarely between a man and wife?
Rarely between parents and grown children?
I am not satisfied about that.
I pound my fist on the table! I insist
That I am not satisfied! I put
My fist through the wall, angrily,

Making a hole. It is
Only in my mind, but
I am trying to force an entry—to deny
That art is illusion, that love is illusion, that
The amusing construction painted with the ruby hearts
Is solid iron, in the gallery.

In Spring Rain

The sodden graves, below their windy puddles,
Feel gratitude. When it clears, a running moon
Sings like a girl. Rocks, where they jut, glisten.

This patient circling, this great vaporous wheel,
This tedium, of a ghostly self obscenely
Thrusting, in April, its itching sensitive fingers,

Wet, pulpy, hopeful. All the while, gray verticals
Aimlessly drop to the earth, and heaven effaces
Itself, for as long as the baby's birth requires.

You go for walks in the rain. It does not matter
That you shiver and make fists deep in your pockets,
That your face is wet. You cross a flooded street,

And the freshness insinuates, despite the batteries
Of your resistance, which so easily
It conquers, seeping, in gusts, like a mild kiss.

Moon and Earth

Of one substance, of one
Matter, they have cruelly
Broken apart. They never will touch

Each other again. The shining
Lovelier and younger
Turns away, a pitiful girl.

She is completely naked
And it hurts. The larger
Motherly one, breathlessly luminous

Emerald, and blue, and white
Traveling mists, suffers
Birth and death, birth

And death, and the shock
Of internal heat killed by external cold.
They are dancing through that blackness.

They press as if
To come closer, to obtain
A reunion. What divides them

Will always be invisible as glass.
The girl will always appear to be serene
As a young actress. She does not shed a tear.

The blue-clad woman moans,
Sings to herself, and following
The daughter's distant

Movements as best
They can, back and forth, in turbulence
Or in calm, rising and falling,

Her waters
Make the image
Of everything.

II

To Kill the Dove

You can go at it either way, said the gentleman
In the study chair. Correctness, propriety, perfection
Should follow from sufficient life,

As we see if we glance
For an instant at the natural world, the cosmic
Or microcosmic, staggeringly (as Whitman warns)

Perfect in least detail, the aphid in dew,
The timid microbe swallowing,
The sheer gleam of the tetrahedral virus.

Unfortunate. Now, taking the converse angle,
If we begin with perfection,
The life following, it will be dry,

Perhaps, but true to life. It will be like a dry,
Glittering spring afternoon. Everything
Is in the most cheerful colors,

Like an actor, with cold lake-blue eyes,
And a smile of infinite charm, to the iceberg teeth,
Of whom we know that he is stupid,

That the attractive appearance signifies nothing,
For example, yet there it is, we fall in love.
And here is the sadness

I want to communicate, whispered the sour gentleman.
Remember, please, this is the twentieth century,
The comfortless.

We all, prone on the grass on a warm morning,
May think of some sprinkling of saints,
Billowed as pigeons, as if a

Hand let go the dust, and the wild wind was passing
Across, and then this was over, this adventure.
And I am getting to it.

To live in a time when the most developed minds
Open and close their papery suitcases.
I am getting to it, he said.

To acknowledge:
Coarse and gross our attachments, our pleasures, our sufferings,
Delusive our recollections, that landscape of breasts,

That history of song behind the ears, that calling, that floating.
To cease the quest for these,
Again, to rest, to close the eyes, to kill the dove.

Downstairs

When he walked downstairs
Into the ground

The final thing he noticed
Was some girls jumping rope down the street

And then the blue-white
Light steadily faded.

It smelled strange there at first
Among the roots, the hairs

The dirt-crumbs, worms, dankness—
Strayed bits of concrete—

At first he thought it like an Edgar Allan Poe story,
And it should have been gloomy and terrifying,

But no, there in the soil and wet
Everything and everyone showed friendship

Where he placed his hand,
Where he rested his forehead.

Ceremony of the Box

Of his own free will he worked on this for many years.
At last he was to present the finished product, which
We may conceive as a plain rather heavy box
Such as he could hold in front of himself with two hands.
As he left, passing under the cedar lintel into the breezy air,
A fist struck him on the right side of the face, another at
The back of his neck, another in the gut. It seems that
Knives and clubs might have been involved as well.
We see him stagger forward and lean over the broad porch
Railing, so that the vomit which pours torrentially from
His mouth, and contains wrenches, needles, playthings
Such as plastic blocks, gloves, artichokes and small
Mice, suspended, and as it were frozen in the stream,
Appears to fall directly upon the grass of the garden below.

The Call

In the world of rain
Where no words are
I am a prisoner of my breath.

            D.F.

Rain does not freshen
Their lives this summer.

The house stays hot.
Wasps fatten on the ripening pears.

He goes in and out
With his briefcase

Awaiting the call
From another world to show him

A way to live without harm.
She and the children

Wallow in it
But his lungs hardly wish to work.

At night they quarrel
Although it is too humid to quarrel.

If nothing happens
He will grow to assume

The air of broken stalks
And their smokeless fume.

The Demonstration

They would lie down on the tracks as a demonstration
Against war and for love, and were to meet at dawn.
Under the old gray station dome stood many policemen
And a small but growing crowd of curious onlookers.
In the mild morning streets, activity began like a noble tune.

"As I would not be a slave, so I would not be a master," they sang.
"The State is like a tree," sang the sergeant, whose face resembled a bathtub.
"Energy is eternal delight," they choraled. "Liberty, equality, fraternity."
"Should old acquaintance be forgot," responded, in mellow baritone, the sergeant.
"Swords into plowshares!" they cried, holding hands, like parts of a long equation.

When everything was ready, the Engineer emerged.
"Sir, I will not go on. Tyranny, like hell, is difficult
To resist. I agree with these people." The leaders instructed them once
More in relaxed breathing and how to be arrested, and they placed
These instructions in the heart of buttercups each wore by the left ear.

At ten they heard the commuters within, restless to go to work.
Then they lay down and the train went over them.
One by one their bodies crumpled with a sigh, as if a child
Broke between thumb and forefinger, making a slight pop,
The dried thoraxes of crickets or mantises found in the grass.

The Terrorist Trial and the Games

At the trial, half the people on the stand were maimed,
Had not the use of their arms or legs, or couldn't
Speak properly. This was as a result of police torture.
They told of being in this forest, being beaten and
Receiving electric shock.

When they began to tell these things, the government
Slaps on the "Suppression of Communism" act, which means
That no more such information can be made public.

At Sharpeville in 1960 the people were demonstrating
For bread. There was a food shortage. Families
Were marching, peacefully, but troops were sent in and fired
On the crowd without warning, killing sixty or seventy
People whose bodies were found.

The white South African woman speaking on the radio program,
Who identifies herself only as "Rosemary," has a voice that
Is soft, gentle and low, flutelike and potentially mirthful.
It's incredible, she keeps saying.

But now there is fire in people's eyes, she says.

Games are the most important thing to South Africans, sports.
They are all crazy sportsmen. If people outside would
Boycott South African teams, not let them play, it would make
A difference, murmurs the voice of Rosemary.

National Public Radio, June 1974

This Dreamer Cometh

— And let us slay him, and cast him
into the pit, and we will say, Some
evil beast hath devoured him: and we
shall see what will become of his dreams.

Genesis 37:20

The Reverend is telling the Committee on Assassinations
How he chose this inscription for the gravestone, and
How when he ran to the balcony, after the shot,
Julian said right away, "It's finished."

And it was

Fifteen years ago in Montgomery days
They learned the FBI was tapping their phones.
Then there is silence on my radio
And a Congressman is asking him, Reverend, have you
Any idea why the FBI would want to do something like that.

National Public Radio, July 1978

The History of America

for Paul Metcalf, who writes of its land and language

A linear projection: a route. It crosses
The ocean in many ships. Arriving in the new
Land, it cuts through and down forests and it
Keeps moving. Terrain: Rock, with weapons.
Dark trees, mastery. Grass, to yield. Earth,
Reproachful. Fox, bear, coon, wildcat. Laughter.
These rise gloomily, it kills them, it tames them,
Its language alters, no account varmint, its
Teeth set, nothing defeats its obsession, it becomes
A snake in the reedy river. Haunted, an overcast
Sky suddenly opens and brightens into infinite
And terrifying blue, which it obeys, keeps moving,
Preparing. Behind it, a steel track. Cold.
Permanent. Not permanent. It will decay. This
Does not matter. It does not actually care,
Murdering the buffalo, driving the laggard regiments,
The caring was a necessary myth, an eagle like
A speck in heaven dives. The line believes
That the entire wrinkled mountain range is the
Eagle's nest, and everything tumbles in place.
It buries its balls at Wounded Knee, it rushes
Gold, it gambles. It buys plastics. Another
Ocean stops it. Soon, soon, up by its roots,
Severed, irrecoverably torn, that does not matter,
It decides, perpendicular from here: escape.

A prior circle: a mouth. It is nowhere,
Everywhere, swollen, warm. Expanding and contracting
It absorbs and projects children, jungles,
Black shoes, rain, and blood. It speaks
Too many dark, suffering languages. Reaching a hand
Toward its waist, you disappear entirely. No
Wonder you fear this bleeding pulse, no wonder.

San Juan Waterfront

The balconied hotels present their rock fronts to the roaring sea.
Chests of officers erect to be seen masculine at exercises.
The clifflike shaven jaw of some rich cardiac case.

On the second-floor balcony the cardiac case stands bonily in his
Shirtsleeves, gray head and late eyes, too old now and it's not funny.
What good is the perpetually seductive sapphire water.

This conspicuous sanitarium or geriatric quality. GERONIMO HOTEL.
CARIBE HILTON to the left. A nameless vertical slab—mortuary word—
Next. FLAMBOYAN across the street. And on, they grit their teeth.

Spanish architecture was civilized even in slums, having warm
Tiles, wood, archways, and a relation between building
And vegetation, which the big hotels, lifting their knees, trample.

Those Who Know Do Not Speak,
Those Who Speak Do Not Know

They split up after attending the excellent experimental film
Program, she wanting to attend a meeting which he did not
Wish to attend. The meeting, which was in a church, was almost
Over by the time she arrived. When she returned home, conditions
Were such that she believed a betrayal of synchronicity
And a lapse of energy and love had occurred, involving the fat
Young babysitter they felt sorry for. She
Immediately expressed her anger and disappointment about this, she
Thought, eloquently and artistically, twice hurling
A kitchen knife at the door where he stood on the stairs
From the kitchen. It was a white door and a medium
Sized wooden handled knife. She had never done this before,
Being a usually inhibited person.
                                   He responded to
This performance with loathing and sadness. He sat on the stairs
Behind the door she shut on him. He did feel like beating her up.
They had some further words, which were not important. He was tired.
He closed his mouth, his eyes, and his pores, like curtains.
Finally they went to bed, made medium sized love.
In the morning they had more words. She cried and felt confused.
He was kind, and told her while shaving there were three ways
Of interpreting her behavior: (a) as folly, (b) as a neutral blowing
Off of steam, or (c) as successful drama. He also pointed out that
Such acts on her part never did bring them together, but made her
Very unattractive to him. He suggested that personal anger was
Seldom valid. She sat on the tub and agreed.

                              Then after a
Little while they got undressed and made fantastic love. They did
Something new, of which the particular shape and sensation
Was quite queer to her, but powerful, like caviar or mangoes. It was a
Warm beautiful spring day.

Three Women

She came home from the dinner party
And the cat came in with her. No
Husband was there; he was away, in
California. She had not succeeded,
That evening, in establishing physical
Contact with the man she was attracted
To, who was moral, and also enjoying
Being elusive. This was pretty funny.
Having grown dry from the gin and tonic,
The wine and brandy, the nuts, plus
The dinner, grass (she had brought,
An agreeable guest), cigarettes and
Coffee, she looked around for something
To eat. Taking a round can of herring
In tomato sauce from the cupboard
And beginning to open it, she found
The gray cat standing alert on its hind
Legs at the counter, clawing her hand.
She gave it three pieces of the tomato
Herring, broken off with her fingers.
Then she picked it up and set it
Outside the back door, saying: "Too
Bad, pet, but you are a mere animal."
Orion hung above her. The screendoor
Slammed, and she finished the fish.

*

Long enough, she had lived in this foreign country.
Long enough, though enjoying the convenience,
The liberty, and the easy manner of people, she
Had felt her mother, and all her mother stood for,
Sternly, like a hard magnet, drawing her back.
She made everything pretty in the house, and she
Went to work at the nursery school. But she wanted
To have a baby. It was remarkable how strong, how
Electrical this desire became, once it had established
Itself, coursing its circuit through her at all times.
He, tall and blond, went out and back, sat in his big

Chair, and in the evenings played his clarinet, and on
Weekends climbed under the Sunbeam, tinkering
And getting greasier than God. No, he did not want
To go back to Norway, where they are idiots. And no,
He did not in the least want a baby. Babies destroyed
Marriages. If he wanted anything, he wanted a new
Porsche. And so, after she became, somehow or other,
Pregnant, it was a joke with them and their friends.
Peter, do you want a boy or a girl?
—I want a Porsche, he would say, rubbing his fingers
Through his blond hair and smiling like a gay dog.
And then he would imagine, for them, assisting
At the natural chilbirth. Out would emerge a black
Rubber tire. Meanwhile, she grew quiet and warm
As a ripening thing. On her mind's bureau was a picture
Of a level piece of water between two banks, entirely
Calm, with no ships or boats or anything else on it,
Smooth and flat and flowing. A few weeks before
The baby was born, she woke in the morning and said:
I dreamed I came back home from here.

*

"He's dying! My God, he's dying!" yelled M's mother,
White and almost jumping up and down on the living-
Room rug with terror, tearing at her
Permanent-waved hair with her orange nails,
Tears rolling down her face. M's sister was
On the floor, moaning and embracing him.
And there Papa lay, on his back, moaning and gasping,
His handsome face without color, all its lines
Drawn downward. His hand was beating at his chest.

Not again. Not again. Not again. Not again. Not again.

But could M understand why, as her mother and sister
Whirled ravished by this pain, she herself felt
As when she sucked on her own black, brittle hair: serene?

Walking forward, then, toward her handsome father,
She seemed quite happy and composed. His face so fine,
The naked ears, the soft symmetrical lips, the thin
Mustache. Stepping around the mound of her sister,
Drawing her foot backward like a bowstring,
Leaning into the motion and kicking him
Heavily as possible in the shirted stomach, it
Was clear her entire body was filled with laughter.
So again she drew back her foot like a bowstring,
And without pause kicked him again as he lay
There on the floor. After a moment, he rose,
He unfolded and opened out far above her like a striped
Umbrella slowly opening. He took his belt off and began
To beat her. None of them said a word, and it hurt
Her in one way, but in another way not. She herself
Thinking mostly about his vanished heart attack
And the way it was a fake, and the way she knew it,
Was still laughing and quite serene internally,
Light as a fleet of balloons.

They sent M to stay with her aunt and uncle a week.
Not a single person afterward ever referred
To this incident. Afterward, along the street,
The maples budded, leafed, shook opulently,
Became red, shed foliage and winged seeds.
M was the younger, the uglier daughter.

But she was right, she brooded, yes, she was right.

Two Writers: For J. D.

She is packing her bags meticulously, including
The silk slips and fastidious handkerchiefs
And will fly back to Sacramento tonight, while he is observing
Himself, primarily, in the hall mirror, unbuttoned
Sexily down to the fourth button, raising his arms to brush
The silvery streaks in his hair, looking,

He trusts, like an Italian gigolo. Within the triangular shape
Formed by his arm and head in the glass, he sees her kneeling.
You look like a gila monster, she sobs. She is a writer. How can you
Just watch me like that. My dear, he replies, many things
Happened to me in the years before I met you. Very little
Touches me now. He is also a writer, and feels that she resembles

A newborn giraffe he once saw in the Bronx Zoo,
But does not mention it, shifts his thoughts to Vienna.
She does not give him credit for this courtliness. I want never,
She says, to be like you. The pink shoes in their shoebag,
The Dior shirt caressingly around his chest. A leisurely
Turning and sighing. Nobody wants to, he says, but you will.

The Long Horn

A and Z were having lunch at the Long Horn: cold cuts,
Cheeses, salads. Z had been mentioning certain
Valuable work done for peace and justice. Z said, if it were to
Do over, she might not have married or had children, for they
Inhibited one's work in life. A asked for whom one's
Work in life was done, and added: "Fastidiousness is
An extreme form of piggery."

*

On Monday night the stars were seen to whirl in concentric
Circles around the North Star. In the morning the
Doctors asked the madmen: "Do you want to be cured?
Do you want to be like us?"

*

"Fastidiousness is an extreme form of piggery. For example,
Chaucer's Prioress, fond of dogs."

*

Without particular warning, he became gradually smaller.
His wife was the first to notice, as he had been
Two inches taller than she. Month after month
His stature diminished while his form remained perfect,
And of course they loved each other more than ever.
Everything started to loom, tragically, but what could he do?
After some time, he was able to be held in her hand.
In her palm he could move everything, as he had always done.
She usually kept him, now, in a little box.
By Christmas it was difficult to see him.

*

The dawn expanded across the sky, whitely at first.
From the deep azure well through which vision and thought
Recede indefinitely, shadowed by light punctuations of stars,
The sky flattened and became less profound, more
Palpable and a boundary. Commonly we consider a boundary
As a pale, a fence; limit in flatland. But the sky
Though spherical can also be a boundary. The sky

At night is boundless, melancholy and foolish. As earth
Turns in its pool of space, like a playing whale, the sky loses
Its depth and becomes a spherical limit. The wind comes up,
The birds begin wildly tweeting, the white sky in its purity
And blankness begins to turn blue, and the sun rises.

Like Fruit

"Men are like fruit, best full of juice," she thought.
There was no sound, except his hand rubbing her. Slip,
Slip, slip. He began to breathe heavily, and she did
Also, then she began to pant. She hugged him around
His solid naked body. This time there was steamy
Immersion in a warm bath full of lavender perfumes. The
Next time she began by stroking him, enjoying his hairiness,
And at the same time he was touching her again. Every
Now and then a bird called. It resembled a long
Curve, a train pulling up a forested grade, reaching a
Plateau, and gliding easily downward, at such a distance that
One could hear no engine and only see the thin smoke
Line rising with fatigue. She opened her eyes and looked
At the cabin skylight which they had made of fiberglass, so
That leaf shadows were always stirring on it, never the same
Pattern exactly for two moments in succession. The hill
Outside was mostly beeches and oaks, occasional birches.
The wooden floor under the sleeping bag which they were
Using as a mattress began to hurt. He rolled off of
Her, to her side. She glanced at the window, and
There, framed in bright green, was the white face of
Their younger daughter, A., smiling queerly.

"Mommy," said A., "B. let C. run into the road and a car
Ran him over." Or, "B. forgot to watch C. and he fell
In the pond." Or, "C. fell on a rock and hit his head and I
Think he's dead." Ah, that was finished, then. Farewell,
Farewell: cost Ceres all that pain to seek her through the world.
A door opened and her soul rushed through it, into the narrow
Corridor, which forever now would lead in the one
Forward direction, however it might branch, inconsequentially,
Hung with the lavish tapestries and mirrors.

A bird called every now and then.

III

Message from the Sleeper at Hell's Mouth

for Rachel Du Plessis and Toi Derricotte

I. THE POET TO HER BOOK

When she sings, when she dances, it is asking
How to capture, how to keep, how to give back, unmasking
Beauty, the seed to the sower, the gift to the giver—

Eros, who shoots in every living thing,
Who is baby, father and lover,
Who breaks the grape apart, who makes the grain

Release its green tongue, whom she desires forever—
Although there is no song
Of love that does not sing of suffering,

Although there is no tale that tells of this
That does not tell of its delusiveness,
Go, book, and say this time she conquers.

II. MOTHER

The musicians are tuning their instruments, the weather
Is right for a wedding, sunny and mild.
I must be crazy. I am going to let you die.

What does it mean to be most beautiful,
Most touched with sweetness? Daughter, you are the target
Man aims his knives at,

You are the stripped abandoned mountainside,
You are the perfect scarlet mouth to test
His sedatives, his white white pills.

Do I do nothing? Do I give you the bouquet, tea-roses
And baby's-breath? I am half
Crying, half laughing.

When the march commences you squeeze
My arm, you thread your eyes into my eyes:
Over and over you walk to the edge of a cliff.

III. FIRST SISTER

The mirror tweezes its eyebrows.
This hurts me more, explains the mirror.
I regret some things, says the mirror, very profoundly.
I regret to inform you. I honestly do.

It hands me a flask of *Brut* for my husband,
The bald salesman, the traveler.
It passes me the latest *Vogue*.
I attack the paper with my nail scissors.

Lie down, commands the mirror.
Not better yet? it whispers in a tin psychologist's voice.
Your migraine, darling? The mirror offers a photograph
Of my sister stroking a serpent.

Good morning, says the mirror.
Repeat after me: Envy is a fingernail scraping a blackboard.
Self-pity is the fifth martini. Second
Best is a loser. I like your outfit.

IV. SECOND SISTER

So much gets buried. Probably she remembers
The way I used to push her "over the moon"
On the swing in the orchard whenever she asked.

She remembers how I would braid her hair,
Real carefully, smelling it, and how she would button my dresses
Saying things like "we are stars" and "I am you,"

Which was her kindness, since I am very plain,
And how we promised each other faithfulness
Until death, back then, before they took her and sold her

In cold blood to the stranger. I know she misses
Our old life. "Little volcano," she called me, "little oven,
Hot inside." I am positive she will return.

V. GODDESS

They do not know, none
Understands, he is my Son,
He is mine, mine,

My only fruit,
That girl is a pig
And a prostitute, no right,

No justice
Would favor her but my kindness.
The many seeds

To sort, that is
Knowledge, the fleece to pull
Is courage, the water of death

To bottle, that is power,
Three tasks. If I
Beat her

She will learn, if I insult her,
She will learn.
I will haul her by the hair, closer to me,

Yes, I will tell
How they first found me, gloriously wet,
Riding the ocean, covered with seaweed,

How they named me,
How each one claims to love me,
How my hands burn, but I love nobody.

VI. ONESELF AT HELL'S MOUTH

It wasn't only my sisters
Making me want to see you,
Burn you, after the touching, the tidal kisses.

I knew you would be lovely,
A lane of flowering trees in a man's form, an army,
A ship of silks, fleeing me in hatred,

The scorch mark marring you.
I knew that I would weep, rise and get dressed,
And hunt you through the world.

*

Whatever happened, I said
Yes, and discovered that every
Time I said it I could

See further, more completely.
Yes, I said to my sisters,
It is you my husband wants,

You go leap off that cliff:
For they twisted their hands like worms
Upturned into a light that hurt.

Performing my tasks, one
After the other, I could see the desire
Of the ants, the reeds,

The tower itself to help me,
As if they were my music, I their voice.
I could see your mother's cruelty

Through her red smile, in heaven, where she lives,
Where I am going to live.
When her malice sent me to hell

The swarming dead implored me for a single
Touch, a single kiss.
No, I said.

*

In the last part of my story I saw pure
Evil, a hard bejeweled box of beauty.
It made me sleep awhile and dream.

The place under my breasts became
More restful, like children
Settling down for an all-night game

Of cards or Monopoly
On a screened porch, a summer evening,
The moths and June bugs in a way

Included, but no bother.
Was it myself, then, in this dream, creeping
Up the wire mesh?

Anyway, what is the soul
But a dream of itself? it pictures
A girl pursuing a god

Who is lovely, naked and wounded,
And in her sleep she says
Come soon, with all your arrows.

The Impulse of Singing

for Cid Corman

That journey he made
Because of an intolerable wound
That would not heal on earth, that he willed to heal

Although all called him fool, that journey
Down from song, down to the impulse of singing,
The pure kingdom of hell:

That was a famous visit
And a triumph. He descended. It seemed they melted,
Pitying. But ascending, he could not carry, hurl, rob

His bride back, and *this*, after all, was his object.
Can you imagine how he sang after that?
How bitterly beautiful, before the crazy women ripped him?

Homecoming

We know that nothing
It says is true, necessarily. When the man
Returned, he was still attractive
And strong, after a decade of war and a decade
Of adventure, according to the story.

The wife, Penelope, was a good lay
Even as a young, slender girl, and
Was now a better one, richer, riper.
But he only found this out
After passing tests. First his dog recognized him,

Yap! Yap! then the stooped crone
Who had nursed him,
Then beautiful Penelope. He had to sneak
In, past a hundred swaggering
Male invaders.

Sullen they were, and arrogant, as snakes.
He frowned: rape artists.
Cold was his anger, and incredibly
Loosed was her burden of control at last.
From rock, he became water, and

In terror and tears,
Kill the sonofabitches! Kill them!
She said. And he did so,
He and the boy, together, in her honor,
Or the story says so.

A man is a fool who
Questions his weeping wife too curiously
(While the carcasses pile up) and a woman is a fool
Who thinks this life
Can ever offer safety,

My husband says that, and he happens to be
The man who wrote the brutal but idealistic
Iliad, while I am the woman who wrote
The romantic, domestic *Odyssey*, filled
With goddesses, mortal women, pigs, and homecoming.

The Runner

for Muriel Rukeyser

Sweat glides on the forehead of the gasping runner
Who runs of necessity, who runs possibly for love,
For truth, for death, and her feet are sweltering.

Behind the runner lies a battlefield.
There, the dust falls. Ahead, the narrow road
Eats a plateau, leads into streets and buildings,

A beach, and the excavation of motherly ocean,
Everything under the arch of an innocent sky.
Sweat runnels between the breasts, evaporates,

And the runner, seeing bright bone under brown landscape
Where one of us would see rocks, bushes, houses,
Begins to feel how fire invades a body

From within, first the splinters
And crumpled paper, then the middle wood
And the great damp logs splendidly catching.

Ah, but some moments! it is so like fireworks,
Hissing, exploding, flaring in darkness,
Or like a long kiss that she cannot stop,

And it is heavy for her, every stride
Like pulling an iron railing
Uphill, ah Christ—we would have to imagine Jerusalem,

Dresden, a hurt this hard, like a screen of fire
Rising, continuous and intolerable
Until solid things melt. Then the runner is floating,

She becomes herself a torch, she is writing in fire
Rejoice, we have triumphed, rejoice,
We have triumphed,

Although words, although language
Must be useless
To the runner.

Homage to Dante

He stood as on a station platform, the wind
Hollowly rushing. A dull glare lit things dimly.
Then the wheel paused, and flickering, they told—

Her lips like apricots, like figs, her breasts
Symmetrical as wineglasses, and the soft nude boy
Tossing his restless curls, thrusting his pale

Angular pelvis, his boy-bone, toward her—they told
Dante their story: "It was then Maytime,
When plowmen gladden, and songs of thrushes bathe

The heart with health. We were like children in purity.
We sat reading on a little grassy hill
Spotted with dandelions, as all about us

The landscape stretched peacefully, and God's heaven
Smiled down. Suddenly love flared,
So that with hands of fire, with mouths

And loins of fire, we sought eagerly
To penetrate each other, and we must swear
That we in part succeeded. Stranger, tell those

On earth of our ecstasy and torment." But they
Had never quite stopped moving, and now
Like a train smoothly leaving a station,

Picking up speed, the wind-ring carried them
Away, whirling, until they were lost to view,
As they would whirl forever. Goodbye, waved Dante,

And sickened, and then fainted.

Homage to Matisse

Because one cares above all and only for this presence,
That consoles and rejoices because it is the truth,
Although one regularly lacerates and mocks, although
They smirk, ignore, they are devious, although the boys
Throw their small brother from the roof: because it is
Difficult yet capable of achievement, for example, in plum
And tangerine, with outlines struck wherever the cheerful
Deity of time, space, and form dictates to the wakeful,
Spontaneous and disciplined spirit, because one wishes
The company of these presences rather even than
The satisfaction of greed, because it seems necessary
To suffer loneliness and the fear of insanity, yet time
After time, over such distances, a hand will reach from
Nothing as a friend to prayer, and confirms the existence
Of the continuous banquet, which you recall at once
Recovered by innocent and subtle rage.

In Moscow June 1971 the only question they asked us was
"What about the hippies? What are they doing? What do
They want?" It was impossible to reply. In Moscow
The faces of people on the street were simple and without
Masks, also without style or sex, naked and tired beyond
Anything I had seen. All life seemed onerous, beyond
What I had seen. Government, which ramified like marble
Down to each public deed, was like bad weather. To move
From one morning to one night was bitter labor. An
Intelligent person would empty himself of desire, and so
In the streets at night there were no lovers but many
Alcoholics. Thus when, gone to Leningrad, in the Hermitage,
Matisse, met by accident you embraced me with brotherly glee
In your roomful of freedom and wisdom, I wished to be seizing
These Moscow friends by the hand, to fly with them
Over the country to you and cry "Here! Here!"

There are four bronze women. These are Pythagorean chords.
They are not invented but discovered. The tracks on which
The universe rolls, like a freight train whose engine is
Everywhere and whose caboose is nowhere, must be harmonious.
Although it commonly shows us, devoured by our lack, a
Cardboard body and a face either maniacal or imbecile, in private
One finds it all smiles and excellent humor. Thus the four women
Of Matisse, phases of one woman whom we may call Autumn, Winter,
Spring, and Summer, or whom we may call a stable
Table, stand with their backs to us, their solid hair
Placed down, either resting on one hip or balancing
Evenly on both strong legs. They vary from bulbously
Protuberant to planar. In any case, while their shoulders,
Buttocks, and calves may be superior to our own, it is
Pleasant to recall that they and we are poised, voyaging,
And simply burning, like the inhuman stars.

"Harmony in Red," The Hermitage, Leningrad
"Backs I, II, III, IV," The Hirschhorn Museum, Washington, D.C.

Anecdote with Flowers: 1919

Renoir at the end painting with brushes strapped to his hand—
Arthritic, crippled—his palette aroused "to crepuscular
Pinks, oranges, reds, his nudes ever more voluptuous"—

We imagine him tucking a counterpane under his beard, coughing,
Whispering "flowers" at death; and the plump, middle-class Parisiennes,
The Great War being over, continuing

Their wholesome pleasures, their picnics,
Their flirtations, their baths,
Like roses, like sunflowers, like peonies.

A Minor Van Gogh (He Speaks):

The strokes are pulses: from my shapely cloud
And sky descending to distant hills
And closer hills, there is a far white tower
That rests, and in the foreground a muddy earth
Of ochre and purple strips, here is my soft clay, my
Bushy juicy green in the corner
And my plowman whom I make at
Dawn forever following his horse
Down the middle of the world. The strokes
Rush forward, waving their hats, identical,
All elements alike, all particles
Of Christ's material dancing, even
The shadowed furrow saying *I exist, I live!*
I also live, and make this form of Christ,
Locked in the light of earth, compassionate.

"Landscape with Plowman," Fogg Museum

Waterlilies and Japanese Bridge

He is the drowsy girl who rows "between the sleeping
Vegetations," Mallarmé calls them, "of an ever
Narrow and wandering stream," and he is a sage who drinks
Milk from the breasts of *le bon dieu* himself.

Like every artist, he is good and happy.
Bourgeois as possible, *mes petits*, like a bee.
Regular hours for mealtimes, slumber,
Labor in the poppy-beds, and moreover,
When a man earns three
Or four thousand francs a canvas, then he may
Whimper at some failing weather, or some broken flower.

May slash imperfect canvases, may pile them in a corner
Of garden and burn them, hooting. Like a porcupine, he
Snuffles and roots in the rosebushes, trots
Through the thin bamboo forest, comes to stand at the pond.
Green, and again green, and again
Mysterious lilies speechless on the water,
Pampas grass, willows, poplars, blocking sky.

Regular hours that are to eternity
As bootlace is to boot. Today he is painting
The overpainted bridge.
Penetrate, penetrate.
It is spots, curves, masses,
It is protected heat, it is his Africa and Asia,
In a saucer, in a cupboard. It is admirable,
Like a wife's pregnant belly and a miser's sums.

This is the year he paints the bridge ten times,
Glutton of light, white butterfly among the green and white,
The pink and white, the deep sienna accents.
In nineteen twenty-two the cataracts
Will crawl, a fungus, over his lenses, he will paint red

Mud and whiplashes, and after this, he will fly out
Of himself among the swift canoeing molecules,
The waterlilies bursting like painless bombs
—Is it from him? or around him? His old man's forehead
Garlanded.

Claude Monet, "Waterlilies and Japanese Bridge," 1899,
Princeton Art Museum

For the Daughters

A god can do it. But how, answer me, shall
A woman follow him through the narrow lyre?
Her head is twofold. At the intersection
Of two heartroads, no temple stands for Apollo.

Song, as you gather it, is not desire,
Not some requirement you may finally fill.
Song is being. For the god, trivial.
But when *are* we? And when does he deliver

To our existence here the earth and stars?
This isn't it, young girl, your love, even
If your voice explodes your mouth—learn

To forget all you sang out. It vanishes.
To sing in truth, there is another breath.
A breath for nothing. A flight in god. A wind.

Adapted from Rilke, "Sonnets to Orpheus"

IV

The Diver

Giving the self to water, a diver
Lifts from stone, sails through air,
Hits, goes under.

Now she remembers everything, this cold
Sweet privacy, the instantaneous
Loss of her name. She remembers that drowning

Is a possibility, like not drowning.
She opens her eyes. Light
Ripples. It is clean

As a birth, a wedding, a suicide ahead
In somebody's life, a chain of jewels. It moves
Freely above the glinting gravel

Of the bottom,
Fathoms away, and as she also moves,
It makes her glad to think about that.

Nobody laughs, under the surface.
Nobody says the diver is a fool.
They are all up above, standing in the heat,

And she would like to call
Up to them, come on in,
The water's fine.

Instead she extends her arms and kicks her feet.
The bottom comes closer,
The diver's body is saying a kind of prayer.

The Pure Unknown

At this time every year I speculate:
What thing, what virtue makes September weather
More pure, more elevating even, than what

Happens in April, when crocus, hyacinth, clover,
Maple and walnut buds are emerging like babies,
Slippery, from their stiff mothers?

The fact of the matter, I admit it, is
This lush and gorgeous foliage I have admired
Is about to burn and die, yet happiness

Makes my step brisk, makes my head
Seem independent of the neck and shoulders, clears
The lungs. It is definite as wood,

And maybe the thing is like reading *King Lear*
Or *Crime and Punishment* when I was seventeen
And knew nothing of despair,

But shivered with tragic bliss, being keen
To race through walls, to experience all
Conceivable human passion,

To be a broken man, while still a girl?
Or later, at eighteen, the levitation
Reading Aquinas, the geometrical feel

Of a towering leafless forest at entrance, or Dante
Canto One, the system of the world
About to be made plain

To me once and for all?
Is it in fact the virtue of the pure unknown,
Boldly announced, through clear air, like a bell?

Like an Orphan

Like an orphan, perpetually insecure and exiled from the soul, B. learned
Much of Shakespeare, could quote scene and line, and would sometimes
Barricade friends who worked in shops, reciting for them the splendid
Passages, the deaths, the exhortations. There was a daintiness of
Spirit, there—vitality—but each day became part of some accumulation
Of bricks, perhaps to wall over a forbidden cellar opening, or perhaps
To load onto an old crumbling wheelbarrow. The eyes of B. were brown,
Large, and serious, with beautiful long lashes.

B. married someone who was gracious and gentle and had a good sense of
Humor, but who secreted a yellow poisonous fluid on the inside: like
A clay bottle or jar.

Over the years B. developed a brilliant bouquet of fetishes concerning
Germs, money and food. These screamed gradually at higher and higher
Pitch. The father whom B. loved for his humble luminousness died slowly.
Later, when the yellow fluid rose to the neck, the mate keeled over.
By this time the children were gone, carrying their sufferings with them
In black imitation-leather portmanteaux, which had always been kept in a
Kitchen cabinet covered with grease, next to evaporated milk.

Like a royal tree after a storm and dead calm, B. began to dance. The
Dance was stationary, yet expressed at once without any seeming effort
Or knowledge the shapeliness of growth from the stiff roots that gripped
Rock, up through solid trunk boughing everywhere outward, smiling; and
Tempo of wind puffs. Another, standing by, played instruments. Still
Others, instructed, plumed their branches curvaceously, the pale undersides
Of their leaves sweeping about in the fresh breeze of this exhilarating
Autumn.

for my mother

The Blood

He closed his mouth like a door. The blood of the chicken was there.
And his mother had his hand tightly. Then he sat at
The table plucking his blue shirt, drinking cream soda.

He said the words in Hebrew. Teacher returned to the room
From the butcher shop, and touched his shoulder. In the avenue
A Ford drove quickly, and there was the small dark stain on his shoulder.

There, he would go to the neighborhood playground, and play
Basketball with the colored boys. He was always smiling.
But his wife saved eggshells. The eggshells were in

An old milk container, and the mucous in them was drying.
She would peel the membranes off them to eat. She would
Save newspapers. He did not wish her to come to Coney Island.

He wished to ride the subway to Coney Island with his child.
The child would whirl on the Steeplechase Amusement Park rides
A summer's day. Sighing at night on the boardwalk they would see fireworks.

What was the mystery? Love swayed his weary clothing.
He was always smiling. When he had to meet a rich man
He was embarrassed. In due time, he would make his heart clot.

for my father

Ceremony of Houses

A row of grand houses facing a river
Glows in the afternoon sun. There is still no chill
In the air. It is Indian summer.

At play in the park, along the sunlit river,
Run children and parents, lovers, collies and strangers.
Calls ascend from their lips, like green balloons,

Higher and higher on the air currents. The maples
Redden. A boy looks up, wanting to fly,
Or to float the way a balloon does, resisting nothing.

When the sun goes down and the park empties,
The houses keep their assurance,
The dark assurance of elders, who question nothing.

Dream: The Disclosure

> Now we see through a glass darkly, but
> then face to face: here I know in part but
> there I shall know even as I am known.
>
> *Corinthians 13:12*

If I would further than I have
Passionately disclosed/disclothed to you
The purple shapes fruits under my skin

  and if we were to lift my unneeded skin
  to discover these convexities—
  pointing the finger, as if we are in biology—

The organs in their refreshing waterfalls of blood
That bathe them nestled lying together and
As you touch this channel you are dislodging jewels

Rubies pearls and diamonds, as each drops another forms, just as
I reached within you beginning at the
Moist cool anus and felt upward until my whole arm

Was enclosed and I felt your bowels
Your stomach your heart shaped elegantly like a pear
My hand cupped round continuing its labors

This was so nice would you drink anything warm
Offered foaming to you in a wooden bowl, by outstretched hands
The juices are harmless, they are not poison, they are life.

The Voices

This happens when I am driving
Fast, or swimming, or skiing.
Always when I'm alone.
The voices want to talk.

They say I have slid away from my history
The way the spirit of a dying person
Struggles out and floats up
To the ceiling

Until its hair brushes the plaster
Of the hospital cell.
They explain that this is what
The spirit does.

It glances out the window
At the traffic and apartment buildings,
Half-smiling, as a woman
Might look at a girl in rhinestones.

It gazes at the sighing relatives,
The eager apparatus,
The white shoes of the nurse, tracking,
And the imminent corpse,

The way we look at earth from an airplane,
Except there's no motion
And no sound
But a slight drum-tapping.

It hovers and shakes its head,
How foolish, how foolish,
And for awhile it climbs back into the body
To help it through to the end.

Dreaming of Her

Outside the longhouse, in a black and drizzling night,
Although I have tightly bolted all the windows,
A woman glides through weeds and struggles to enter.

Her gray hair falls in her face.
Her breasts are many years milkless, threadbare
Pockets. Her skirt is dragging, and danger

Beams from her vacant womb. When the building
Shifts in the wind, my children hide, and she stands
Next to me, quiet, on the naked wood floor.

I am furious. *Who let this witch in?* Then she's gone.
My children creep out, staring.
And we hear her step in the mud, pound at the window.

All night the orange moon crosses the sky,
Rain comes and goes, the dream repeats, repeats—
Mother, sometime we are going to talk

Together, I promise—And when I wake I am crying
Peacefully onto the pillow, in clear morning,
As if it were I, my mother, released from the black

Hunger of daughterlove. As if it were I.

Don't Be Afraid

This is when I want to open you
Like a sweater, like a jacket

That you have kept closed,
To walk into your heart

As if it were a major avenue
In an unpolluted city, and I could hike

From one end of the city to the other
With all I own on my back,

Breathing the fresh
Air of your heart, looking at clouds and buildings.

The Courage

for L. W.

Caught in the snow
One impulse is

To bow your head,
To keep going, but slowly,

Letting the flakes fall on your hair
And your naked neck,

Letting the snowflakes pile up
On the shoulders of your old wool coat.

Oh you could hug yourself
With cold

While the sky grew hollow
As the statues in all the parks

And the wind blew around you
Like your twin brother's spirit.

You would hear the hissing
Across curbstones and car roofs

And no other sound
For many miles.

A Woman Walking in the Suburbs

October stillness and the last leaves hang
Golden on the trees.
All month I strained to become
Luminous and transparent as the leaves
And I failed. Indeed, I grew thicker.
Now, having relinquished, I succeed,
My breathing and needs decrease,
I am quite tranquil. I feel the light fly through me.

It is too late. I intended to show the man, only
He has rumbled away, an engine down its track.

Here is a slip of a child, coming along
With me, holding my fingers and kicking the leaves.
We see the dark gray damp spots under them,
And what a peaceful
Afternoon it seems to be.
We see the swingset in the children's playground
And another lonely woman walking a dog.
Westward, our red sun sets.

The man was my sun. The shining he cannot see now
Flows with all fairness.

Storm

The sky became the color of a bruise.
We hid from it, as you would, we rose up and up
On the vomited wave.

The winds hurtled us, slammed us, constantly.
We tore each other's clothing; fell, wrestled,
Clung and screamed. We were ready to die,

Or murder, anything, packed in like slaves.
We remember the furry stink, the pandemonium,
The dipping in blackness.

But the dead were outside, drowned and weltering.
Hundreds of packs of picture cards
Flung from some high window onto a river,

Waterlogged, bloated, sunk. Unbreathable rottenness
Climbed the strings of rain like ivy, until we
Scraped, grated, stopped.

A shocking sky, motionless and blinding.
A mocking orb.
We will never forget this adventure,

Neither the scars nor the anger,
Nor fresh air mingled with steam,
Nor airy colors. It is because of this thought

And cross-thought, our capacity
For it, that we were saved.
Now all the living beings

Fan out, away
From us, across
The lumped, cratered skin of our earth,

Faint, fainter, trails of an explosion.

Anxiety about Dying

It isn't any worse than what
I discover in the dentist's chair
Under the nitrous oxide.

The whole jaw is going, I complain, the gums, the bone,
Two enormous fillings just last week. What do I need?
How about a guillotine, says my dentist, the joker.

The only thing I have to fear is fear itself, I tell him.
You believe in that bullshit? he says,
Setting to work on my rotting bicuspid.

Now comes the good part. Breathing the happy gas
I get answers to all the questions I had
About death but was afraid to ask.

Will there be pain? Yes.
Will my desires still be unsatisfied? Yes.
My human potential still unrealized? Yes.

Can a person stop minding about that? Certainly.
Can I commend my spirit to the seventeen
Angels whistling outside the dentist's window?

Of course. How nice the happy gas.
What a good friend.
I unclench my sweaty little hand.

I wave goodbye to my teeth.
It seems they are leaving by train for a vacation.
I'll meet them in the country when I can.

The Singing School

First they asked you to step through the many rooms
Until you came to the one where Father waited
Wearing his old chinos and sneakers.
It was painted eggshell. Two cups of coffee stood
On a rosewood table, and the night air blew
Pleasantly in at a half-open door.

He told you about his journey through a tunnel,
Saying that he was frightened.
Only he winked at you and laughed
About it while he talked.

Another time they set you in a blizzard
And you were wearing layers of heavy clothing.
With each removal of clothing the snow lessened.
Then finally you were naked, an August sun
Caressing you, and dragonflies were gliding
Above an oval pond . . .

Now you know how to sing.
Now you have to make
Your own story.

A NOTE ON "MESSAGE FROM THE SLEEPER AT HELL'S MOUTH"

The story of Eros and Psyche in Apuleius' *Golden Ass* begins with Psyche, a maiden so lovely men worship her instead of Aphrodite. The goddess orders her son Eros to punish Psyche, but instead he falls secretly in love with her. An oracle declares that on her wedding day Psyche must be dressed as for a funeral and left at a cliff's edge. This is done, and she is wafted to a palace, where her mysterious husband, visiting her nocturnally, makes her vow never to try to see him. Psyche is happy but becomes homesick and obtains permission to see her sisters. They, hearing her tale, tell her she has wed a monster; she must light a lamp when he sleeps, see his true self, and prepare to kill him. When Psyche does so she discovers that her husband is the God of Love, and is overjoyed. But oil from the lamp burns him on the arm; he wakes, deserts her, and the palace vanishes.

Psyche returns to her sisters, announcing that Eros bids them leap from the cliff to be his new brides; when they do so they are killed. She then sets out in search of Eros, and receives help at every turn. Aphrodite gives her several impossible tasks, which with assistance and advice she performs. Finally she must descend to Hades and obtain from Persephone a box of beauty for the goddess. A tall tower tells her how to go about this task: she must not try to aid the dead who will accost her, and she must not open the box. Psyche completes the task successfully, but when she leaves the mouth of Hades, opens the box. From it comes a miasma that puts her to sleep. It is at this point that the gods intervene, Eros retrieves Psyche, and she is granted immortality.

Library of Congress Cataloging in Publication Data

Ostriker, Alicia.
    A woman under the surface.

    (Princeton series of contemporary poets)
    I. Title.   II. Series.
PS3565.S84W6   811'.54   81-47938
ISBN 0-691-06512-8   AACR2
ISBN 0-691-01390-X (pbk.)

Alicia Ostriker is Professor of English at Rutgers, The State University of New Jersey.